# OUR BABY
## A BIRTH AND ADOPTION STORY

# OUR BABY
## A BIRTH AND ADOPTION STORY

Written by JANICE KOCH
Designed by PAT GOLDBERG

**PERSPECTIVES PRESS**
FORT WAYNE, INDIANA

Published by    Perspectives Press
                905 West Wildwood Avenue
                Fort Wayne, Indiana 46807

Manufactured in the United States of America

ISBN 0-9609504-3-5 (hardcover edition)
ISBN 0-9609504-4-3 (softcover edition)

Library of Congress Cataloging in Publication Data

Koch, Janice, 1947-
  Our baby.

    Summary: Explains how babies are created by birth parents and how some parents adopt babies to be their very own.
    1. Adoption—Juvenile literature.   2. Human reproduction—Juvenile literature. [1. Adoption. 2. Reproduction] I. Goldberg, Patricia J., 1939-  ill. II. Title.
HV875.K94 1985          362.7'34          85-6392
ISBN 0-9609504-3-5
ISBN 0-9609504-4-3 (pbk.)

TO ROBIN AND BETSY

**FOR** _____

place child's
picture here

This is a story about **you.**

How you were **born** and how your Mommy and Daddy **adopted** you for their own **special child.**

A long time ago, well before you were born, Mommy and Daddy met each other.

They felt a **special** way about each other and that feeling grew into **love.**

They chose each other to spend the rest of their lives **together.**

Mommy and Daddy were **married** and they lived very happily together.

After a while, they decided that they
wanted a **child** of **their very own**
to share their lives with.

There are **two** ways that grownup
people become **mommies** and **daddies.**

One way is to **grow** a baby of their own. Another way is to **adopt** a baby of their own.

**Your** Mommy and Daddy **adopted** their baby — **You!**

Every **new person begins** as a tiny seed which grows inside a woman's body.

**You** grew inside a woman's body too.

A man and woman **start** that tiny
seed that produces a new person by
using certain parts of their **bodies.**

The man and the woman who started
you were your birthparents.

A **woman's** body produces a tiny **ovum** once every month. It is so small, that it is just about the size of a pinhead.

A **man's** body produces many,
many tiny **sperm** that are released
from his penis. The tiny **sperm**
cannot be seen unless you use a
microscope.

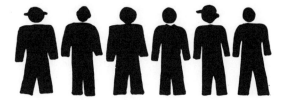

The tiny **sperm** can reach the small **ovum** inside a woman by entering the woman's vagina and swimming up toward the ovum.

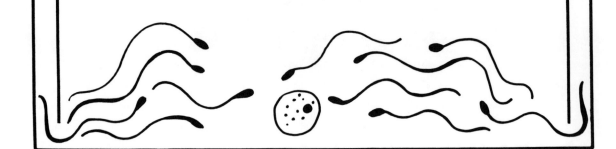

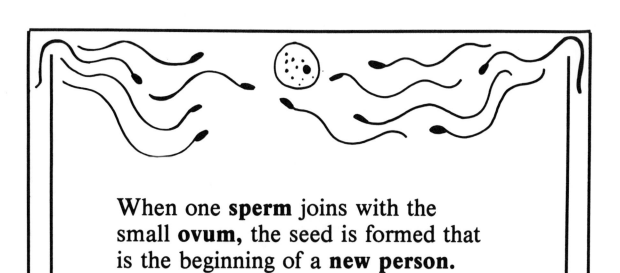

When one **sperm** joins with the
small **ovum,** the seed is formed that
is the beginning of a **new person.**

**You began this way.**

At the very beginning the seed is called an **embryo**. As it grows inside a woman, it gets bigger and bigger and then, it is called a **fetus**.

The part of the woman's body that the growing **fetus** lives in is called the **uterus.**

It takes a very long time - nine months - until the fetus is ready to come out of the woman's body.

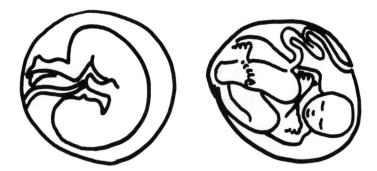

When it is ready to be **born,** it comes out of the vagina of the woman and it is a **newborn baby.**

This **newborn baby** is like **you** when **you** were **born.**

Mommy and Daddy spoke to a special person who knows about **babies** that are going to be **born** and people who want to **adopt babies.**

One day, this person called Mommy
and Daddy to say, **"There is a baby
that you may adopt."**

And that **baby** was **you!**

Many people want very much to
adopt newborn babies.

Mommy and Daddy are very happy
that **you** became part of our family
after you were born.

Some mommies and daddies meet the baby that they are going to adopt at the **hospital** where the baby is born, others meet their babies at **adoption agencies** or at **airports**.

We met you at _____

when you were _____ old.

Mommy and Daddy brought you home and fed you special baby milk from your bottle and watched as you slept in your crib.

As you grew bigger, you learned to do so many things. You learned to **crawl** and then **walk** and even **talk!**

Before long you were big enough to have **stories** like this one read to you!

Mommy and Daddy wanted you so much. We are so happy that you are **our baby** and that we are **a family!**

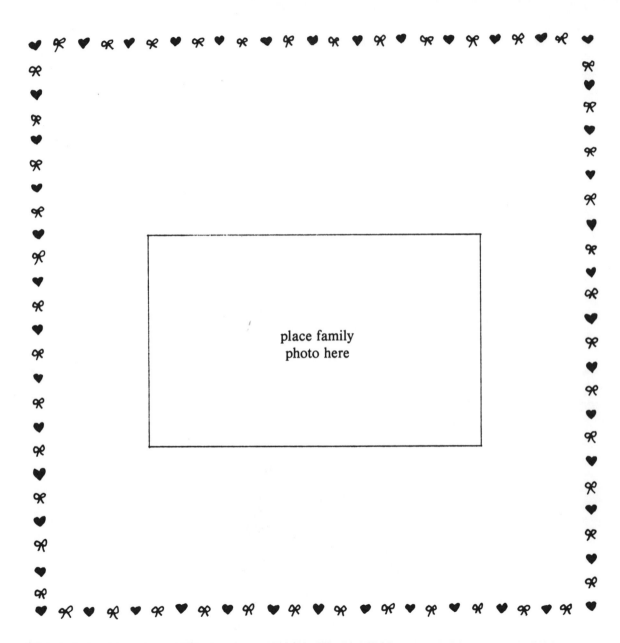

place family
photo here